# HORSES

Grosset & Dunlap

All photographs are the property of Harold Roth, except for photographs provided by All-Sport Vandystadt, page 28, Katey Barrett, page 30; Joseph DiOrio, page 3; and Douglas Lees, pages 22, 23, 31.

Library of Congress Cataloging-in-Publication Data

Roth, Harold.
   [Big book of horses]
Horses: an abridgment of Harold Roth's big book of horses \ text by Margo Lundell, photographs by Harold Roth; abridgment by Laura Driscoll.
   p. cm. —
Summary: Includes information on the history of the horse and its relationship to humans, the diffferent breeds and their uses, how to care for horses, and riding styles and techniques.
    1. Horses—Juvenile literature. 2. Horsemanship—Juvenile literature. 3. Horses sports—Juvenile literature. [1. Horses] I. Lundell, Margo. II. Driscoll, Laura. III. Title.
SF302.R68      1997
  636.1—dc21                                     97-13765
                                                                        CIP

ISBN 0-448-41735-9                    2008 Printing                                    A C

# HORSES

**An Abridgment of *Harold Roth's Big Book of Horses***

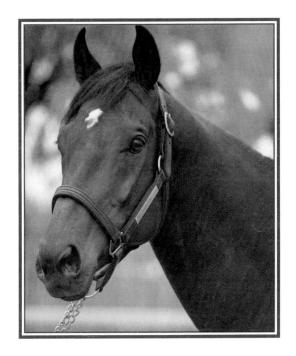

Text by Margo Lundell
Photographs by Harold Roth
Abridgment by Laura Driscoll

Grosset & Dunlap, Publishers

Long ago in America, horses were everywhere you looked—pulling coaches and carriages filled with people, hauling loads from farm to market, and delivering important mail.

Today, we have cars, trucks, and planes that take people and things from one place to another. Even so, we still see horses in many different places—at the fair, the circus, in the park, and running in horse races.

Most horses grow up on farms. A baby horse is called
a **foal**. In just minutes, a newborn foal can stand up and take
some wobbly steps over to its mother. The baby will stay
very close to its mother until it is about six months old.

A one-year-old horse is called a **yearling**. Yearlings are about half as big as adult horses—and twice as frisky!

A two-year-old horse is like a teenager. It is as tall as it will get, but its muscles and its bones are still developing. A horse is an adult when it is five years old.

There are certain things that make horses very happy. Most horses love to run just for the fun of it. In wide-open pastures, they gallop from one end to the other, glad to be out in the open. Sometimes mother horses, like the one in this picture, challenge their foals to a race by running on ahead of them.

Horses like to roll around on the ground. This is just the thing for scratching an itch. It also covers the horse with a thin layer of dirt, which protects against biting insects.

Horses also love to eat—especially oats, hay, grass, carrots, and sugar cubes for a sweet treat. They are called **grazing animals** because they like to eat often, but only a little bit at a time.

Horses come in all shapes, sizes, and colors. It all depends on what **breed** a horse is. A breed is like a family of horses all related to one another.

**Morgan** horses are strong and fast.

**Thoroughbreds** are the fastest long-distance runners of all the breeds. Most racehorses are Thoroughbreds.

**Arabian** horses are famous for their beauty and speed. This is one of the oldest breeds we know of.

Most cowboys had **American quarter horses**. They were the most popular workhorses of the American frontier.

**Appaloosas** come in lots of different colors, but most of them have spots. So sometimes they are called "raindrop horses."

There are many kinds of **ponies**. Some people think ponies are small because they are baby horses. But they are not. All ponies, even adult ones, are small because that is just how their breed is.

Have you ever wondered what it would be like to have your own horse? Here is what an average day might be like.

Bonnie has a horse named Bambi. Early in the morning, Bonnie goes to Bambi's stable. She gives him a hello pat on the nose and some grass to munch on. Then Bonnie cleans the stall. She takes away any dirty straw or sawdust on the floor and puts clean sawdust in its place. The sawdust is a little easier on Bambi's legs than the hard floor.

Then it's time for breakfast. Bonnie brings fresh water,
hay, and oats for Bambi.

Later on, Bonnie gets Bambi ready for a ride! First she **grooms**, or brushes, Bambi.

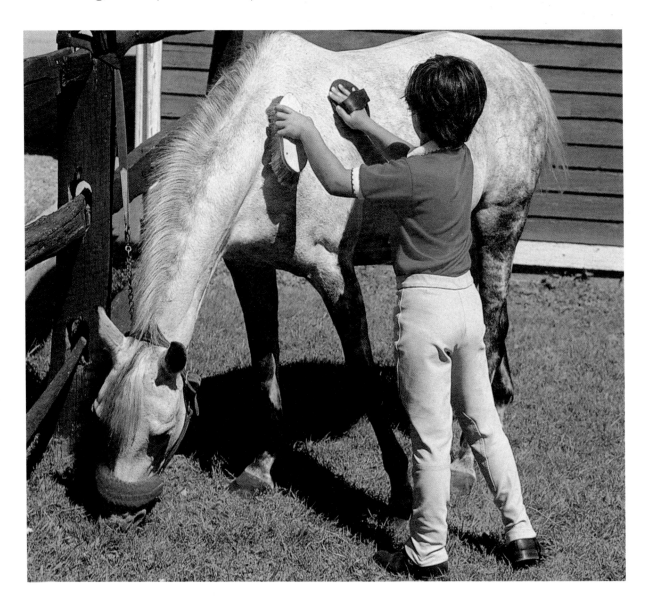

Bonnie also must scrape out any dirt or stones stuck in Bambi's hooves. Otherwise, he could get an infection or sore spots.

Finally, Bonnie and Bambi are ready to saddle up and go. They race down the long meadow together. There are many different ways riders can tell their horses what to do. Sometimes they pull lightly on the horse's reins. Sometimes they press on the horse's sides with their legs. Sometimes they use their voice. Every horse is different, and some like certain signs better than others.

On warm days, Bonnie gives Bambi a little shower after the ride. Then, she lets him graze in the meadow, while she cleans the saddle and the other riding equipment.

At the end of the day, Bonnie brings Bambi back into the stable and gives him dinner—more hay and oats and fresh water. Then Bonnie says good night and leaves Bambi to drift off to sleep in his stall.

Sometimes kids who have their own horses enter them in horse shows. Young riders have to show judges how their horses walk and run at different speeds. In some youth competitions, horses also show off their jumping skills. Jumping takes a lot of practice, but it's one of the most exciting events at a horse show.

In adult competitions, horses and riders jump over high fences, race on cross-country courses, and sometimes perform **dressage**, a series of very exact, small steps. The best horse-and-rider teams might get to go to the Olympics!

And they're off! At horse races, the fastest horses speed around the track at about forty miles per hour! Racing fans flock to racetracks to see the colorfully dressed riders, or **jockeys**, and to cheer for their favorite horses.

This kind of horse racing has taken place for thousands of years. Sometimes it is called the "sport of kings" because many English kings and queens over the centuries have owned horses that they used only for racing.

At a rodeo, riders need quick horses for events like calf roping. The horse speeds after a runaway calf while the rider tries to lasso his rope around it.

Rodeos include events for both male and female riders. In the barrel racing event, cowgirls run their horses as fast as they can in a cloverleaf pattern around some barrels. Their horses must be able to turn very quickly.

What would a cowboy be without a horse? Some ranchers and cowboys round up their cattle the same way they always have—on horseback. Many cowboys have American quarter horses because they can easily scramble up hillsides and swim across rivers.

**Harness racing** is like race walking for horses. They are not allowed to run at full speed, or **gallop**. They must trot toward the finish line as fast as they can. Riders sit in carts called **sulkies** and steer with long reins.

In the game of polo, riders on horseback hit a wooden ball with long-handled mallets. Their polo horses are called **ponies**, no matter how big they are. The best polo ponies follow the ball wherever it goes, without even being told by the rider.

Horses are a big part of the show at the circus. Strong horses pull colorful wagons. Smaller horses circle the ring carrying acrobats on their backs. And beautiful, white horses called **Lipizzaners** can leap and prance just like ballet dancers.

Clip-clop, clip-clop! If you've ever taken a ride in a horse-drawn carriage, you've heard that sound. Before the engine was invented, this was how almost everyone got from place to place. Today, horse-drawn carts and carriages are used mostly for quiet rides through the park or for special occasions.

Horses in parades always look very calm, but it takes a lot of training for them to behave this way. Cheering crowds, whistles, and other loud noises can scare horses. Once a horse has learned to ignore everything but the rider, it is ready to go on parade!

Sometimes big parades include police officers on horseback. Lots of cities have mounted police units. In New York City, they patrol parks and other public areas. Just like parade horses, they are trained to ignore the loud noises of the city.

What would horses be like if they weren't tamed and trained by people? Long ago, all horses were wild animals. They lived and roamed together in big herds.

One kind of wild horse is the **mustang**. Millions of mustangs lived in the American West during the 1800s. But then people began to hunt wild horses, and soon there weren't many left. Today, a law protects all of America's wild horses so they can run free.

There are lots of reasons to love horses! They are gentle, intelligent animals. And people who spend time with lots of horses say they have definite personalities—that each one has a special character and spirit all its own. It is easy to see why horses have always been so important to us, and why they are some of the most popular and well-loved animals of all time.